P9-EME-720
TO:
FROM:
DATE:

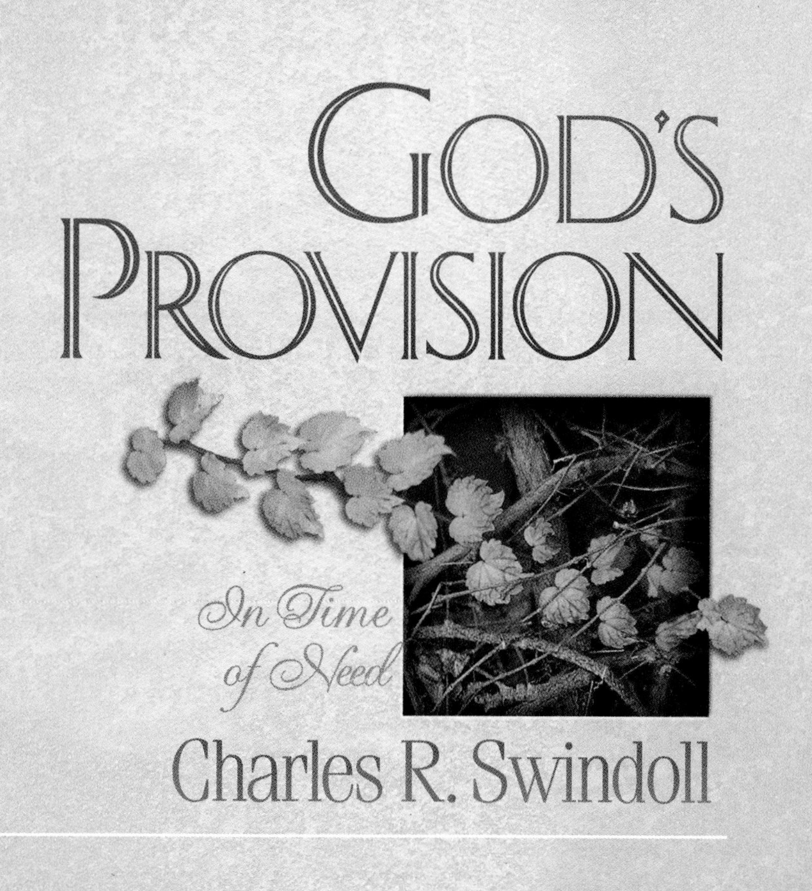
GOD'S
PROVISION
In Time
of Need
Charles R. Swindoll

Published by J. Countryman, a division of Thomas Nelson, Inc.,
Nashville, Tennessee 37214

Compiled and edited by Terri Gibbs

A J. Countryman Book

Designed by Koechel Peterson Inc.
Minneapolis, Minnesota

ISBN: 0849995426 - paperback

ISBN: 0849995434 - paperback se

CONTENTS

GOD PROVIDES...

FOREWORD

We want to be strong. And yet a key principle in the Christian life is that God is never stronger in His work than when we are, admittedly, weak. When we come to an end, He steps up and shows Himself strong.

When times are tough, the Lord is our only security. When days are dark, the Lord is our only light. When our walk is weak, the Lord is our only strength.

Yet, I have observed that we frequently have trouble believing God is our only hope, security, light, and strength because we are so prone to try everything else. We automatically depend upon everything except the Lord. Yet still He waits there for us—patiently waiting to show Himself strong.

He is our light and our salvation; whom should we fear? He hears our cry. He lifts us up out of a horrible pit; He places our feet upon a rock and establishes our going. He proves Himself strong in our weakness; He sheds light in our darkness; He becomes hope in our uncertainty and security in our confusion. He is the Centerpiece of our lives.

So let's be strong—in the Lord!

CHARLES SWINDOLL

GOD
PROVIDES...
Relief for Stress

Old Jethro frowned as he watched Moses dash from one person to another, one need to another. From morning until night Moses was neck deep in decisions and activities. He must have looked very impressive—eating on the run, moving fast, meeting deadlines, solving people's problems.

But Jethro wasn't impressed. . . . He told Moses:

Call for Help. . .

The world beginning to get you down? Too tired to pray? Ticked off at a lot of folks? Let me suggest one of the few four-letter words God loves to hear us use:

Help!

In this race called life, when the pressing demands of time are upon us, we need to stop and get oriented. We need to discover that the Lord is God. He will be exalted; He is with us; He is our stronghold.

When you're pressed, when you're under stress, when you're pushed down and your weakness is displayed, God is building a tent of refuge. He's protecting you; He's surrounding you with His custodial care and strength.

In extreme assaults of stress, God invites us to rest in *His eternal embrace.*

When was the last time you flew a kite, took a long walk in the woods, pedaled a bike in the local park, drove *under* the speed limit . . . or strolled along the surf at sunset?

God's Provision in Time of Need

Every one of us can blame somebody
for something that has happened in our lives.
But don't waste your time.
What we need most is a steady stream
of love flowing among us.

The hand of God holds you firmly in His control.

The hand of God casts a shadow of the cross across your life. Sit down at the foot of the cross and deliberately submit your soul to His mighty hand. Accept His discipline. Acknowledge His deliverance. Ask for His discernment.

. . . Then be quiet. Be still. Wait.
And move over so I can sit beside you.
I'm waiting too.

When you do what is right,
without tiring of it, God takes care
of the impossible things.

I will hold you up, God says.
But as long as you lean on someone else,
you can't lean on me.

If you live in light of Christ's return each day of your life, it does wonders for your perspective. If you realize that you must give account for every idle word and action when you stand before the Lord Jesus, it does amazing things to your conduct. It also makes you recognize how many needless activities we get involved in on this earth. Sort of like rearranging the deck chairs on the *Titanic*. Don't bother! Don't get lost in insignificant details! He's coming soon!

I never cease to be amazed at how perfectly God weaves His will together without our help!

God's Provision in Time of Need

What if you're not getting the raise or the promotion you deserve? What if you are in a situation where you could make things happen . . . but you really want God to do that?

Think of David, the young musician, tending his father's sheep back on the hills of Judea many centuries ago. He was a self-taught, gifted musician. He didn't go on tour, trying to make a name for himself. Instead, he sang to the sheep. He had no idea that someday his lyrics would find their way into the psalter or would be the very songs that have inspired and comforted millions of people through long and dark nights.

David didn't seek success; he simply humbled himself under the mighty hand of God. . . . And God exalted David to the highest position in the land.

The beautiful thing about this adventure
called faith is that we can count on God
never to lead us astray.
He knows exactly where He's taking us.
Our job is to obey. . . .

God always knows
what He's doing.

One of the best ways I know
to keep from getting angry
when we don't get our way
is to have a good sense of humor.
Turn the bad times into a little fun.

Those who wait on the LORD
Shall renew their strength;
They shall mount up with wings like eagles,
They shall run and not be weary,
They shall walk
and not faint.

Isaiah 40:31

Those who wait upon
the Lord will gain new strength.
But remember: The key to the
Lord's strength is *waiting*.

When I keep my
hands out of things,
God's will is accomplished,
His name is exalted, and
His glory is magnified.

GOD
PROVIDES...
Assurance for
Worry

God's Provision in Time of Need

Jesus dropped by His friends' home in Bethany. He was, no doubt, tired after a full day, so nothing meant more to Him than having a quiet place to relax with friends who would understand. However, Martha, one of the friends, turned the occasion into a mild frenzy. To make matters worse for her, Martha's sister Mary was so pleased to have the Lord visit their home that she sat with Him and evidenced little concern over her sister's anxiety attack. . . .

Mary's simple faith, in contrast to her sister's panic, won the Savior's affirmation.

What is wrong with worry? It is incompatible with faith. They just don't mix.

Our English word *worry* is from the German, *worgen*, which in that tongue means "to strangle."

Worry takes all the bad news on TV and puts us in the middle of it. Jesus, however, calmly takes our shaking hands in His and tells us not once, but twice:

"For this reason I say to you, do not be anxious for your life, as to what you shall eat; nor for your body, as to what you shall put on. . . . Do not seek what you shall eat, and what you shall drink, and do not keep worrying."

Luke 12:22, 29

Worry, fear, and selfishness are our mortal foes. They keep us from seeking God first. They pin down our spirits and take our minds captive with horizontal thoughts.

Don't contaminate today by
corrupting it with tomorrow's troubles.
Refuse—yes *refuse*—to allow tomorrow's
lagoon of worries to drain into today's lake.
Today is challenge enough!

When you face an impossibility, leave it in the hands of the Specialist. The things which are impossible with men are possible with God.

Luke 18:27

Our problem is that we hold onto our problems.

Worry drains our energy and makes us tired, because prior to the actual battle, we fight the Enemy a hundred times in our minds. . . . Relax. Untie those knots of anxiety with the settled assurance that the Holy Spirit will be there in your moment of need.

When our future
is foggy or fuzzy,
the Lord is
our only hope.

The energy and effort we expend worrying never solves a thing. In fact, it usually makes the situation worse for us, creating a terrible inner turmoil which, if allowed to intensify, can paralyze us. . . . Even when trials are pressing in and people are trying to intimidate us, we can have a calmness of spirit.

. . . How?
Because we know
that God is on
our side.

We just take life
one day at a time.
That's the way God dispenses life.
Because He never changes and
He knows what will work
together for good.
You and I don't.

Ever have something begin to kind of nag you? You can't put your finger on it. It's fuzzy. Sort of a slimy ooze. It's just growing in the corner, nagging you, getting you down. That is the beginning of a heavy anxiety. We need discernment to detect it, identify it, and get to its root so we can deal with it. When we see the beginning of anxiety for what it is, that's the precise moment to cast it on God, to roll that pack on Him.

God is never at a loss to know what He's going to do in our situations. He knows perfectly well what is best for us. Our problem is, *we* don't know.

There is no impossible situation that God cannot handle. He won't handle it necessarily your way,

but He'll handle it.

God sees our need to trust Him, and His love is so great that He will not let us live another day without turning over our . . . fears, our worries, our confusion, so that nothing becomes more significant to us than our Father.

GOD PROVIDES...
Strength for Temptation

No sin, save the sin of Adam and Eve, has received more press than the sin of David and Bathsheba. Moviemakers exploit the passage with their "David and Bathsheba" films, conveying the idea that this man was some sort of a sexual addict with uncontrollable animal-like drives. That's not true. That's not true at all. This is a good time to remember that David was a man who loved God. . . . He was still "a man after God's heart." He sinned, but his sin was no greater than your sin or mine; ours simply have not been recorded for all to read.

Self-control is an ingredient from heaven that God gives us when the Spirit of God lives within and controls us. But . . . we are to "supply it."

On the heels of a mistake, get on your knees, fall before God, and lay out your shame and humiliation. No one else can heal you of that sense of shame. . .

—no one.

There is no creature hidden from His sight,
but all things are naked and open
to the eyes of Him
to whom we must give account.

Hebrews 4:13

Nothing is hidden from God's sight.
Everything is laid bare to His eyes—and still
He sympathizes with us!

If you want to stay clean, even when you're walking alone in the dark, low-ceilinged coal mine of the corrupt and secular culture, you need to remember a few practical things:

1. Pay close attention to what you look at.
2. Give greater thought to the consequences of sin rather than to its pleasures.
3. Begin each day by renewing your sense of reverence for God.
4. Periodically during each day focus fully on Christ.

Not even becoming a Christian erases our imperfections. We still make mistakes—even dumb mistakes. But, thank God, forgiveness gives us hope. We still need a lot of it.

God's Provision in Time of Need

Contrary to popular opinion, God doesn't sit in heaven with His jaws clenched, His arms folded in disapproval, and a deep frown on His brow. He is not ticked off at His children for all the times we trip over our tiny feet and fall flat on our diapers.

. . . He is a loving Father,
and we are precious in His sight,
the delight of His heart.

If you want to be a person with a large vision, you must cultivate the habit of doing the little things well. That's when God puts iron in your bones!

We can decide to walk with God and draw strength from Him to face whatever life throws at us. Or we can decide to walk away from God, and face the inescapable consequences.

We think of love as something that is giving, but sometimes love involves taking away something that would not be best.

GOD
PROVIDES...
Peace for Fear

Her name was Esther. She was the Jewish wife of a Persian king, the man who was about to be tricked into making an irrevocable, disastrous decision. All Jews would be exterminated. . . .

Esther's adoptive father, realizing that she, alone, held the key to her husband's heart, appealed to her conscience. . . .

She broke long-standing protocol, marched into the king's throne room, spoke her mind . . . and rescued the Jews from holocaust. . . .

She didn't think, *Someone else should be doing this, not me* . . . nor did she ignore the need because of the risk. She was willing to get personally involved, to the point of great sacrifice.

Few things are more persistent and intimidating than our fears and our worries . . . especially when we face them in our own strength.

The fierce grip of panic
need not immobilize you.
God knows no limitation when it comes to
deliverance. Admit your fear. Commit it to
Him. Dump the pressure on Him;
He can handle it.

What then shall we say to these things? If God is for us, who can be against us? . . . Who shall separate us from the love of Christ? Shall tribulation, or distress, or persecution, or famine, or nakedness, or peril, or sword? As it is written: Yet in all these things we are more than conquerors through Him who loved us. For I am persuaded that neither death nor life, nor angels nor principalities nor powers, nor things present nor things to come, nor height nor depth, nor any other created thing, shall be able to separate us from the love of God which is in Christ Jesus our Lord.

Romans 8:31, 35–39

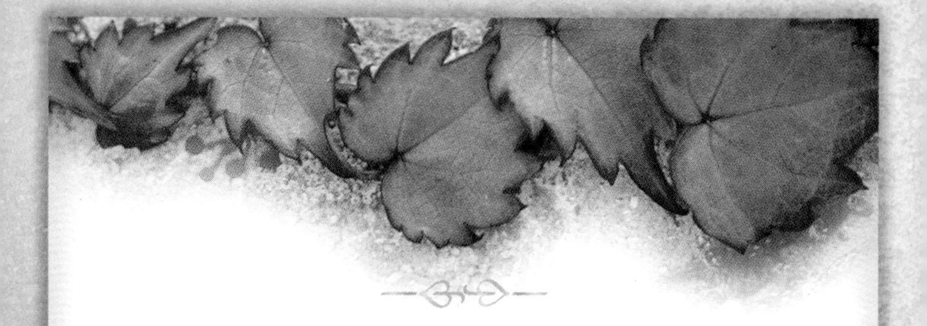

Entrust.

What a wonderful word! It is a banking term . . . meaning "to deposit." . . . When it comes to trials, we deposit ourselves into God's safekeeping and that deposit yields eternal dividends.

. . . When you deposit money in the bank, there's a limit on how much the FDIC will insure under one account ownership; usually it's about $100,000. But our infinite God has no limits. Millions upon multimillions of Christians can deposit themselves in His care, and He will make every one of them good. He will hold every one of us securely.

Leaving the details of my future
in God's hands is the most
responsible act of obedience
I can do.

Our sovereign Lord operates from an eternal agenda, not a daily planner. Sometimes, when we expect Him to charge over the hill with the cavalry, He holds back. Other times, at the exact moment we think He has misplaced our address, He comes in through the back door. And when we wonder if we'll ever feel His warmth, He pulls us in from the cold and sets us in front of His crackling fire. . . .

Even with all He has revealed about Himself in His Word, His hand often moves in ways we can't explain.

If we will only believe and ask,
a full measure of God's grace and peace
is available to any of us.

To trust God completely requires the
discipline of surrender.

Trust in the LORD with all
your heart, and lean not on
your own understanding;
in all your ways acknowledge Him,
and He shall direct your paths.

Proverbs 3:5–6

We can face *whatever* life throws at us when our strength is sourced in God.

God gives us just enough light so that we can see to take the next step. That's all He gives and, in reality, that's all we need.

It is God's love for us that causes
Him to bring us to an end of our own strength.

God doesn't give temporary relief.
He offers a permanent solution.

To cultivate serenity,
it is imperative that we guard the
discipline of solitude.

GOD
PROVIDES...
Hope for Trials

God's Provision in Time of Need

Paul had a thorn in the flesh, and he prayed three times for God to remove it.

"No," said God, "I'm not taking it away."

Finally Paul said, "I've learned to trust in You, Lord. I've learned to live with it."

It was then God said, "My grace is sufficient for that thorn."

He matched the color of the test with the color of grace.

You can't carry yourself through the storms; it's too much for you. When will we come to the realization that the blizzards in our lives are allowed by God? Those threatening storms are designed to slow us down, to make us climb up into His arms, to force us to depend on Him.

As a result of God's mercy, we have become a people who are uniquely and exclusively cared for by God. The fact that we are the recipients of His mercy makes all the difference in the world as to how we respond to difficult times.

. . . He watches
over us with
enormous interest.

The Lord dispels

His angels of hope who bring invincible help, because He finds delight in us. He cares for us. He feels our ache. He feels it deeply.

For of His fullness we have all received, and grace upon grace.

John 1:16

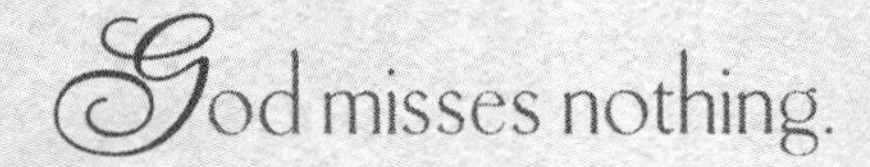

He's looking out for us.
He's listening to our prayers.
And He is completely aware of the
evil that is happening to us. . . .
But if this is true, we wonder,
why doesn't He do something about evil?
Why does He let it go on so long?

. . . In the end,
count on it, God will be just.

In the end,
He will "work everything
together for good"
and for His glory.

Anybody can accept a reward graciously, and many people can even take their punishment patiently when they have done something wrong. But how many people are equipped to handle mistreatment after they've done right?

...Only Christians
are equipped to do that.

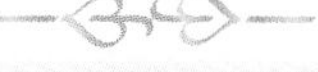

The common response
to trials is resistance,
if not outright resentment.
How much better that we open the
doors of our hearts and welcome the
God-ordained trials as honored guests for
the good they do in our lives.

Trials are not an elective in the Christian-life curriculum; they are a required course. Trials 101 is a prerequisite to Christlikeness.

You're just standing there, and suddenly the smooth lake of your life surges into giant waves and almost drowns you.

. . . If you're experiencing trials, you're the rule, not the exception. If you have just gotten through one, take heart; there are more around the corner! Going through a trial is one thing that pulls us together. We've got that in common.

We are never
closer to the Lord,
never more a recipient of His strength,
than when trials come upon us.

Our major goal in life is not to be happy or satisfied, but to glorify God.

When the sovereign God brings us to nothing, it is to reroute our lives, not to end them.

Life is a schoolroom.

In it, we encounter pop quizzes and periodic examinations. You can't have a schoolroom without tests—at least I've never seen one. . . . Throughout the educational process our knowledge is assessed on the basis of examinations. The curriculum of Christlikeness is much the same. Our Christian maturity is measured by our ability to withstand the tests that come our way without having them shake our foundation or throw us into an emotional or spiritual tailspin.

. . . The wonderful thing about God's schoolroom,

however, is that we get to grade our own papers. You see, He doesn't test us so He can learn how well we're doing. He tests us so *we* can discover how well we're doing.

God's Provision in Time of Need

Some of you are going through trials right now that have dropped you on your knees. At the same time those trials are pulling you closer to the Lord than you've ever been in your life. That ought to bring rejoicing. You'll be more closely linked to Him.

When God says "no" it is not necessarily discipline or rejection. It may simply be redirection.

God's Provision in Time of Need

At the height of one of his own personal tests, Hudson Taylor expressed his response in these words: "It doesn't matter how great the pressure is. What really matters is where the pressure lies, whether it comes between me and God or whether it presses me nearer His heart."

When we are pressed near the heart of God, He is faithful and He will hold us. He will hug us through it.

If you know a real test is coming,
talk to the Lord about it.
Then trade off with Him.
Hand over your fragility and receive
His strength in return.

GOD
PROVIDES...
Grace for
Suffering

God's Provision in Time of Need

An old Hebrew story tells of a righteous man who suffered undeservedly. He was a man who had turned away from evil, took care of his family, walked with God, and was renown for his integrity. But suddenly, without warning, and seemingly without reason, he lost everything he had: his flocks, his cattle, his servants, his children, and finally his health. This old Hebrew story is no fairy tale. It is the real account of a real person—Job.

Though he suffered terribly, and though he could never have foreseen it himself or understood it when it happened, Job has been remembered down through the ages and to this very day as a model of patient endurance.

Suffering is the common thread in all our garments.

Living through suffering,

we become sanctified—in other words, set apart for the glory of God. We gain perspective. We grow deeper. We grow up!

God seems to reward us with good, delightful experiences when we move with joy through those times when we didn't get our own way.

When you are hurting, you need to declare it to someone, and especially to the Lord.

We can rejoice through suffering
because we have a permanent inheritance—
a secure home in heaven.

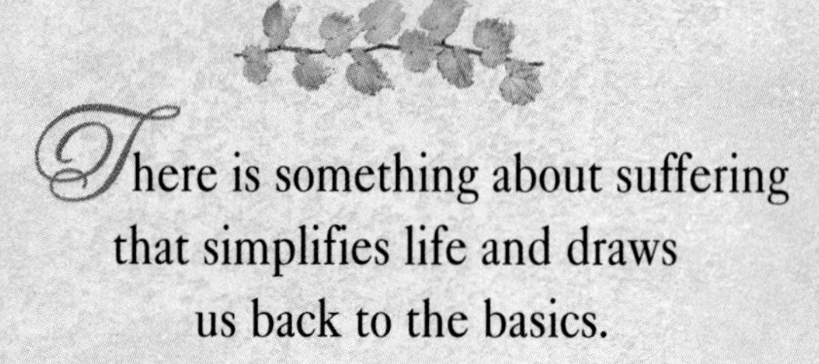

There is something about suffering
that simplifies life and draws
us back to the basics.

"If when you do what is right and suffer for it you patiently endure it, this finds favor with God."

1 Peter. 2:20

The word *endure* in verse 20 means "to bear up under a load," as a donkey bears up under the load its owner has stacked high on its back. This patient bearing of life's cumbersome loads is made possible by love, made steadfast by hope, and made easier by example.

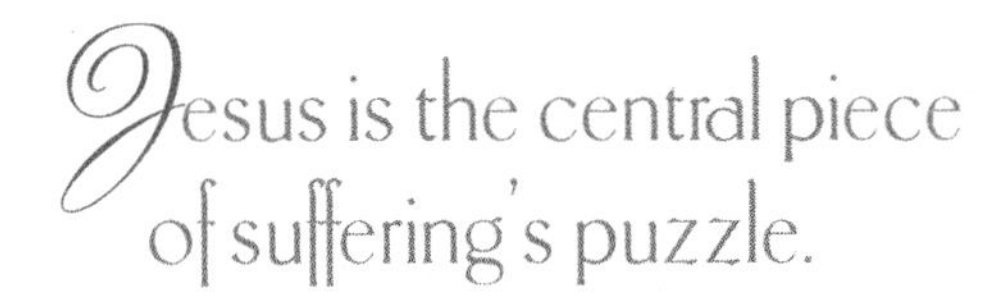

Jesus is the central piece of suffering's puzzle.

If we fit Him into place, the rest of the puzzle—
no matter how complex and enigmatic—
begins to make sense.

When you suffer and lose, that does not mean you are being disobedient to God. In fact, it might mean you're right in the center of His will. The path of obedience is often marked by times of suffering and loss.

The furnace of suffering provides not only light by which to examine our lives but heat to melt away the dross.

When we are suffering, only Christ's perspective can replace our resentment with rejoicing.

GOD
PROVIDES...
Comfort for Sorrow

When [Stephen] gave an eloquent and penetrating defense of Jesus before the Jewish Sanhedrin, this infuriated many who heard him. Their hatred raged out of control. Do you remember his response? . . .

Stephen didn't deserve their savage attack. He certainly didn't deserve death. Because of that, he could have died in bitterness and cynicism. He could have died with curses on his lips. Instead, he sanctified the moment to God and died with a prayer on his lips, asking forgiveness for those who so mercilessly killed him. When those men looked into Stephen's face, they didn't find their own hatred reflected back at them; they saw the reflection of the Savior's grace and love.

God offers special grace to match every shade of sorrow.

Even when life is dreary and overcast, rays of hope pierce through the clouds to stimulate our growth. In fact, without pain there would be little growth at all, for we would remain sheltered, delicate, naive, irresponsible, and immature.

When times are tough, the Lord is our only security.

It's hard enough to deal with the consequences of our own missteps, miscalculations, and stupid mistakes. But it seems unbearable to suffer the consequences of something that wasn't our fault or that we didn't deserve.

. . . Like quicksand,
feeling sorry for ourselves
will suck us under.

Has a friend betrayed you?

Has an employer impaled you?
Has a disaster dropped on your life that's almost too great to bear? If so, don't fight back. Unjust suffering can be a dizzying experience. To keep your balance in those times when things are swirling around you, it's important to find a fixed reference point and focus on it. Return to the protection and guardianship of the Good Shepherd who endured the cross and laid down His life . . . for you.

When God develops character,
He works on it throughout a lifetime.
He's never in a hurry.

Be strong in the grace
that is in Christ Jesus.

2 Timothy 2:1

Love is the pillar of support
when our world comes crumbling
down around us.

It is not a sign of weakness and
immaturity to have a friend or to need a friend.
It's a sign of immaturity to think
you don't need a friend.

When life hurts
and dreams fade,
nothing helps like hope.

The price paid for us was unimaginably high—the blood of Jesus Christ—and now we belong to Him. . . . That's enough to bring a smile to anyone's face.

GOD
PROVIDES...
Forgiveness
for Failure

We can learn a lot from Peter, a man who spent over three years with Christ and who . . . both pleased Him and failed Him. In fact, most of us should be able to identify with Peter. He'd been an eager disciple, defending his Master against all comers. He'd also been a failure, denying his Lord in the pinch . . . not once, but three times, back to back. Through all this, God reshaped him into a powerfully effective man of God. The vacillating, impulsive, overly zealous Simon was changed and broken, emerging as "Peter, the rock."

You are of infinite worth to God. You're worth so much to God that He sent His Son to die for you.

I've never met anyone who became instantly mature. It's a painstaking process that God takes us through, and it includes such things as waiting, failing, losing, and being misunderstood—each calling for extra doses of perseverance.

God helps the helpless,
the undeserving, those who
don't measure up, those
who fail to achieve
His standard.

Since Jesus Christ our Lord is the same yesterday and today and forever, then we can take the Christ of today and walk with Him into our yesterday and ask Him to remove the pictures that bring bad or defeating memories.

. . . We need to let Him leave
the murals that bring pleasure
and victory and take down from
the walls those things that bring
despair and defeat.

The next time you begin to think how unworthy and wormy and inferior you feel, remember that to God you are the object of His attention and His affection.

If we confess our sins, He is faithful and just to forgive us our sins and to cleanse us from all unrighteousness.

1 John 1:9

For I know the thoughts that I think toward you, says the LORD, thoughts of peace and not of evil, to give you a future and a hope.

Jeremiah 29:11

Those who have
never recognized their own
failures have a tough time tolerating,
understanding, and forgiving
the failure of others.

God's Provision in Time of Need

Often when we are faced with a crisis, the standard, garden-variety answer is to sort of tuck your tail between your legs, run into a corner, and let cobwebs form on you. But there is a better way. As long as you have breath in your lungs, you have a purpose for living. You have a reason to exist. No matter how bad that track record might have been . . . you're alive, you're existing. And God says, "There's a reason. And I'm willing to do creative things through you to put you back on your feet. You can lick your wounds if that's your choice. But there's a better way." It will take creativity, it will take determination, it will take constant eyes on the Lord. But when He pulls it off, it's marvelous.

There is no
counsel like God's counsel.

No comfort like His comfort.
No wisdom more profound than the
wisdom of the Scriptures!

God is ready to fill your empty hands like you would never believe if you will only lift them up to Him in obedience and praise.

The truth is that all of us are needy people, it's just that some of us hide it better than others.

What we often don't realize is that behind the scenes, before He ever flung the stars into space, God had today in mind. He had this very week in mind. In fact, He had you in mind. And He knew exactly what He was going to do. God is never at a loss to know what He's going to do in our situations. He knows perfectly well what is best for us. Our problem is, *we* don't know. And we say to Him, "Lord, if You just tell me, then I'll be in great shape. . . ." But that's not faith. Faith is counting on Him when we do *not* know what tomorrow holds.

Each new dawn it's as if
God smiles from heaven, saying,
"Hope again . . . hope again!"